	HIK265	**RIVERS THROUGH TIME (5 vols.)** ★	94.75
____		LEVEL: GRADES 5-7	
____	HI526X	Settlements of the Ganges River/Spilsbury, Spr 05	18.95
____	HI7182	Settlements of the Indus River/Bowden, Spr 05	18.95
____	HI7190	Settlements of the Mississippi River/Bowden, Spr 05	18.95
____	HI720Y	Settlements of the River Nile/Bowden, Spr 05	18.95
____	HI7212	Settlements of the River Thames/Bowden, Spr 05	18.95

RIVERS THROUGH TIME

Settlements of the River
NILE

Rob Bowden

Heinemann Library
Chicago, Illinois

Customer Service 888–454–2279

Visit our website at www.heinemannlibrary.com

Photo research by Ruth Blair and Ginny Stroud-Lewis
Designed by Richard Parker and Tinstar Design Ltd (www.tinstar.co.uk)
Printed in China by WKT Company Limited

09 08 07 06 05
10 9 8 7 6 5 4 3 2 1

Library of Congress Cataloging-in-Publication Data
Bowden, Rob.
   Settlements of the River Nile / Rob Bowden.
      p. cm. -- (Rivers through time)
   Includes bibliographical references and index.
   ISBN 1-4034-5720-4 (hardcover) -- ISBN 1-4034-5725-5 (pbk.)
1. Nile River--Juvenile literature. I. Title. II. Series.
   DT116.B69 2004
   962--dc22

                              2004002426

Acknowledgments
The publishers would like to thank the following for permission to reproduce photographs:
Alamy pp. 18, 43; Ancient Art and Architecture Collection pp. 19, 31; Axiom p. 21; Corbis pp. 4, 5, 11, 15, 17, 33, 37; Corbis pp. 34, 36 (Paul Almasy), 25 (Yann Arthus Bertrand), 14 (Lloyd Cluff), 27 (Digital Image/NASA), 20, 30 (Robert Holmes), 9 (Michael Nicholson), 12 (Carmen Redondo), 29 (Reza Webistan); Images of Africa pp. 39, 40, 41; Pictures p. 42; Robert Harding p. 23; Still Pictures p. 13; Sylvia Cordaiy p. 39; The Art Archive pp. 24, 35.

Cover photograph reproduced with permission of Picture Colour Library.

Illustration: Stephen Sweet (SGA) and Jeff Edwards

Contents

Words in bold, **like this**, are explained in the Glossary.

Introducing the River Nile

The majestic Nile

The River Nile is the longest river in the world. It stretches for an incredible 4,132 miles (6,650 kilometers) and passes through seven countries. The Nile is actually two rivers—the White Nile and the Blue Nile. They join to become a single river, the Nile, at Khartoum in Sudan. In this book, we focus on the White Nile because this is the longer of the two rivers. It also has more **settlements** along its length than the Blue Nile does.

In addition to being the king of rivers, the Nile is also called "the river of kings." This nickname refers to the **pharaohs** of ancient Egypt who ruled the Nile Valley for thousands of years and built great kingdoms. The remains of these kingdoms still exist in modern-day Egypt. They include the pyramids of Giza near Cairo and the temples and Valley of the Kings in Luxor. The ancient Egyptians thrived along the Nile because of its life-giving waters. Every year the river would flood and deposit a layer of thick, **fertile** soil across the Nile valley.

This is an ancient Egyptian wall painting of a husband and wife plowing fields by the River Nile (shown at the bottom of the picture).

River glossary

Confluence: the point where two rivers join.

Delta: where the river joins the sea.

Mouth: the ending point of a river.

Reaches: sections of the river (upper, middle, and lower reaches).

River course: the path followed by a river from source to mouth.

Source: the starting point of a river.

Tributary: a river or stream that joins another, normally bigger, river.

The rich soils brought great harvests to the farmers of the Nile valley. The Nile also provided a trade route between the Mediterranean Sea and the heart of Africa. Such goods as ivory, gold, and spices were traded up and down the river.

The Nile is as important to the people living along it today as it was in ancient times. It still provides water for farming and is an important transportation route. The Nile brings new benefits, too. These include electricity generated by the force of its waters and tourists who come to wonder at the river, its people, and their history.

From source to mouth

Although people have lived along the Nile for thousands of years, its **source** remained a subject of great mystery until 1858. That year, British explorer John Hannington Speke identified the start of the White Nile as Ripon Falls in present-day Uganda. Here the Nile flows out of an enormous lake that Speke named Lake Victoria after the British queen of the time. However, further explorations have shown that the ultimate source of the Nile is the Kagera River in Burundi. It is from here that the Nile is measured as the world's longest river.

In its upper **reaches,** the White Nile switches between a crashing, fast-moving river and a much slower, more gentle one. The fast-flowing sections are caused by a series of rapids, where water crashes over hard rocks that lie across the riverbed. The slower sections form much wider channels of water. In northern Uganda, the White Nile drops over the Kabalega Falls. It then carves its way through the mountains of southern Sudan before almost slowing to a halt in the Sudd. The Sudd is a giant swamp full of vegetation that clogs the river and sends its waters spilling over the level land around it.

In its middle reaches, the White Nile leaves the Sudd and flows slowly for around 500 miles (800 kilometers). In Sudan's capital, Khartoum, the White Nile is joined by the Blue Nile, which begins at Lake Tana in the highlands of Ethiopia. After cascading over Tis Abay Falls, the highest on the Nile at 148 feet (45 meters), the Blue Nile cuts through the highlands in deep gorges. The fast-moving waters carry thousands of tons of **sediment** with them as they **erode** the land around them. Although shorter than the White Nile, the Blue Nile contributes about 70 percent of the water that eventually flows into Egypt.

Downstream of Khartoum, the river is simply known as the Nile. It is joined by another major tributary, the Atbara River, before it reaches Egypt. Today, the Nile enters Egypt through Lake Nasser. This lake was formed by the Aswan High Dam, which holds back the Nile and controls the release of its waters into Egypt. Below the dam the Nile passes through a narrow valley with desert on either side of it. Shortly after passing through Cairo, the Nile splits into two channels known as the Damietta and Rosetta. Once there were seven channels, but over time water has been diverted into just two so that more land can be used for farming and for settlements. These form the **delta** region of the Nile, where the river eventually meets the Mediterranean Sea.

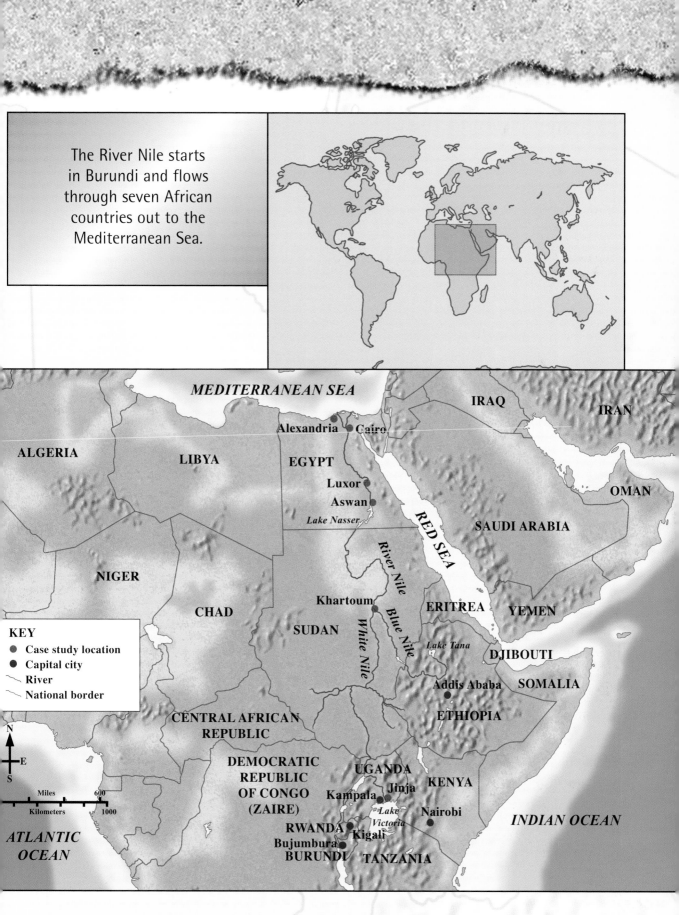

The River Nile starts in Burundi and flows through seven African countries out to the Mediterranean Sea.

MEDITERRANEAN SEA

IRAQ

IRAN

Alexandria • Cairo

ALGERIA

LIBYA

EGYPT

OMAN

Luxor

Aswan

SAUDI ARABIA

Lake Nasser

NIGER

River Nile

RED SEA

CHAD

ERITREA

YEMEN

Khartoum

Blue Nile

SUDAN

Lake Tana

DJIBOUTI

White Nile

KEY
● Case study location
● Capital city
⟋ River
⟋ National border

Addis Ababa

SOMALIA

CENTRAL AFRICAN
REPUBLIC

ETHIOPIA

N
E
S

DEMOCRATIC
REPUBLIC
OF CONGO
(ZAIRE)

UGANDA

KENYA

Kampala   Jinja

Miles   600

Kilometers 1000

Nairobi

Lake Victoria

INDIAN OCEAN

RWANDA

Kigali

**ATLANTIC
OCEAN**

Bujumbura
BURUNDI

TANZANIA

Settlements along the Nile

The Nile has settlements along most of its length except for the mountainous stretches of its upper reaches. Most of these settlements are small farming and fishing villages located close to the banks of the Nile. A few of these settlements have developed into larger towns where people gather to trade goods. In Uganda, for example, Jinja has become a major market for farm produce and for fish caught in Lake Victoria.

Most of the major settlements along the Nile lie in its middle and lower reaches. For thousands of years, much of this region was flooded each year by the annual flow of the river. As the flood waters subsided, they left behind a fresh layer of **nutrient-**rich sediment carried down from the Ethiopian highlands. This provided the best farmland in all of Africa, and the farmland attracted settlers. The Nile also provided water for farming and homes and a transportation route for the movement of goods and people. Today, the annual flooding of the Nile is controlled by a series of dams. However, the river is still a major center of population from Khartoum to its **mouth.** The Nile is surrounded

What's in a name?

*The River Nile is known by many different names from source to mouth. In its first section, for example, it is known as the Victoria Nile, while in southern Sudan it is known as Bahr al-Jabal, meaning mountain Nile. The ancient Egyptians knew the river as Ar or Aur, which means black. It was called this because of the black sediment that was carried by the river when it was in flood. The modern name, Nile, is thought to have developed from a **Semitic** word nahal, which means river valley. In Greek this became Neilos (Nilus in Latin) and over time this changed to give the name Nile.*

by desert on either side, and the river provides a narrow strip of life through this barren landscape. Great cities such as Cairo, Alexandria, and Khartoum control this area, but there are hundreds of smaller settlements in between, such as Aswan and Luxor.

In this book, we will explore the major settlements along the River Nile. We will follow a journey through time, starting with Aswan and ending in Jinja—a town where plans are being made that may change the Nile forever. We will look at why these settlements were founded and how they have changed. We will consider what those settlements are like today and how they might change in the future. Most importantly, we will discover how the settlements are linked to the Nile and the lives of the people living there.

The calm waters of the Nile pass through the center of Cairo— the largest city in Africa.

Aswan: The Great Dam

City of elephants

It is difficult to say exactly when the first **settlement** appeared at Aswan. One thing is certain, however; it has been settled for a very long time. Some of the earliest records for Aswan suggest that it dates back to at least 3000 B.C.E. Whatever the precise date, Aswan has always been an important center for trade. Its name comes from the ancient Egyptian word *Swen,* which means "market." Aswan was in a perfect location for trade because it was the farthest point south that boats could reach by sailing up the Nile. A set of rapids, known as the First Cataract, blocked their passage further upriver. The ancient Egyptians believed that these falls were the Nile's **source**.

The earliest settlement at Aswan was on an island in the middle of the Nile called Elephantine Island. This unusual name comes from its ancient Egyptian name, Abu, which means "elephant." Some experts think this refers to the granite boulders in the water around the island that look a bit like bathing elephants. Others believe that the island was once an important center for trading ivory.

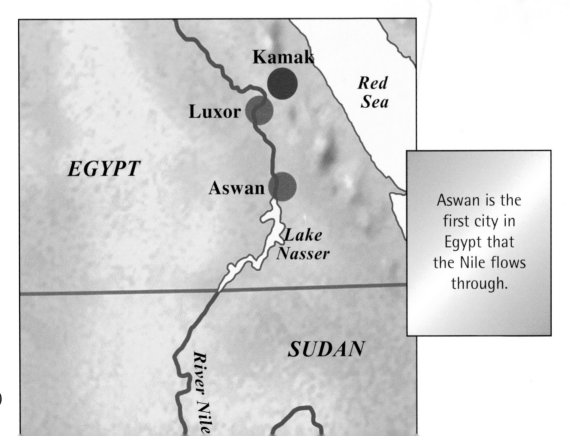

Red Sea

Kamak

Luxor

EGYPT

Aswan

Lake Nasser

SUDAN

River Nile

Aswan is the first city in Egypt that the Nile flows through.

Traders also brought gold, leather, precious stones, ebony, and spices. Elephantine Island became an important southern capital for the Egyptians. Not only did it bring the riches of Africa, it also provided a base to protect Egypt from southern invasions. Most importantly, however, the island was located where it was easy to monitor the annual flooding of the Nile. This was done using a device known as a Nilometer.

A Nilometer is a steep staircase cut into the side of the island and down into the Nile. The 90 regularly shaped steps acted as markers to measure the rise and fall of the river. The level of the flood recorded at the Nilometer was used to predict the future harvest in the Nile valley downstream. This helped the Egyptians figure out the amount of tax that farmers had to pay to the **pharaohs.**

Today, Elephantine Island and its Nilometer are major tourist attractions. **Archaeologists** are also working on the island to learn more about the ancient origins of Aswan. They are slowly unearthing the remains of an old town at the southern end of the island. This has revealed a temple to Satis, a goddess linked to the Nile. Her husband, Khnum, the lord of the Nile flood, was believed to guard the waters of the Nile at this point of the river.

11

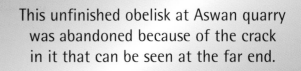

This unfinished obelisk at Aswan quarry was abandoned because of the crack in it that can be seen at the far end.

Land of granite

Aswan played a key role in the construction of many of Egypt's greatest temples. It was the main source of granite, a hard rock used to build many of their finest buildings. The granite around Aswan was valuable because of its many different shades—gray, black, red, and even pink. The pyramids at Giza (see page 31), which were built between 2613 and 2494 B.C.E., were some of the first to include granite quarried around Aswan. Once cut from the quarry, the granite was taken downstream by boat along the Nile. Without the river it would have been almost impossible to transport such heavy pieces of rock.

The most impressive pieces to be transported by river were two giant **obelisks.** An obelisk is a square-sided pillar that narrows to a point at the top. The obelisks were built by Queen Hatshepsut, who ruled Egypt between 1490 and 1468 B.C.E. She ordered that they should be carved from a single piece of Aswan's best pink granite. A team of workers took seven months to complete the obelisks. Each stood nearly 99 feet (30 meters) tall and weighed 323 tons. The obelisks were transported to Luxor by river and were placed in the temple of Karnak in 1475 B.C.E. They were the tallest obelisks in Egypt, and one of them still stands in the temple ruins today.

Nile feluccas are part of the scenery around Aswan. Once used for trade, they are now more commonly used to take tourists out on the river.

Another obelisk remains on its side in an Aswan quarry, still attached to the bedrock beneath it. If it had been finished, it would have been the biggest obelisk ever made. It would have stood around 138 feet (42 meters) high and weighed as much as 1,190 tons. It appears that the obelisk was abandoned because a crack developed in the rock as it was being carved. Although unfinished, the obelisk has given archaeologists a chance to see the skills used to create such magnificent objects.

Nile feluccas

The river in Aswan is crowded with graceful sailboats called feluccas. Today, feluccas carry tourists on trips around the islands or from one bank of the Nile to the other. In the past, feluccas would have been the main form of transportation up and down the Nile. As long ago as the time of the pharaohs, they would have transported goods to and from the market in Aswan. Their simple design is so suited to life on the Nile that it has changed little in thousands of years. For many visitors to Egypt, a felucca is still the best way to visit the temples that line the Nile between Aswan and Cairo.

13

Damming the Nile

Aswan is still an important market town in Egypt today. Its market attracts traders who have traveled along the Nile or across the surrounding desert. However, the town is best known for its dams across the Nile. The first dam was completed in 1902 by the British, who were in control of much of Egypt between 1882 and 1952. Although it was important at the time, the old dam is now overshadowed by the Aswan High Dam. This massive dam took eleven years to build and was finished in 1971. It is 2.2 miles (3.6 kilometers) long, and its main wall is 364 feet (111 meters) tall and 3,215 feet (980 meters) wide at its base. Behind the dam, an artificial lake, Lake Nasser, stretches upstream for 310 miles (500 kilometers) into neighboring Sudan.

The Aswan High Dam was considered a great triumph for Egypt. It controlled flooding and provided water for new areas of farmland. The dam also allowed electricity to be

> The Aswan High Dam controls the Nile waters and provides much-needed electricity for Egypt.

3000 B.C.E.	2613-2494 B.C.E.	1475 B.C.E.
Probable founding of Aswan.	Pyramids at Giza are built using granite from Aswan.	Queen Hatshepsut's obelisks transported to Luxor for the Temple of Karnak.

Farming and trading of goods, such as spices, takes place alongside more modern industries in Aswan.

generated by the water passing through the dam. The electricity and the guaranteed water supplies attracted industries to Aswan. Today, these industries include cement production, a sugar refinery, copper and steel factories, and a chemical fertilizer plant. New workers settled in Aswan, and the town's population rapidly grew. Before the dam was finished, Aswan had a population of around 40,000 people. Today, the population is almost 250,000.

The Aswan High Dam is vital for Egypt's economy and its people, especially the millions living downstream of it. Today, around 70 million people are dependent on Aswan and its control of the Nile.

Not all good news

*The Aswan High Dam has not been all good news. When Lake Nasser was formed, the Nubians who once lived in the valley south of Aswan were forced to move. Their houses and many ancient temples were lost beneath the waters. Downstream of the dam, the annual floods no longer carry **nutrients** to fertilize farmers' fields. As a result, farmers now depend on chemical fertilizers. The use of water for **irrigation** has also caused a rise in the **water table** under Egypt's farmland. This has brought salts to the soil surface and has caused declines in crop growth in some areas. The effects of the Aswan High Dam are even felt as far away as the Mediterranean Sea. There, sardine catches have fallen dramatically because nutrients are no longer carried into the sea by the annual Nile floods.*

1882–1952 C.E.	1902	1971
British in control of Aswan.	First dam at Aswan completed by the British.	Aswan High Dam is completed.

Luxor: City of Kings

A royal city

Luxor is at the heart of Egypt's tourist industry. Thousands of tourists visit it every day. They come to see the remains of ancient palaces and temples that once graced this royal city. In ancient times, the **settlement** was actually known as Thebes. This name is sometimes still used to describe the area around the modern town of Luxor. In the early period of Egyptian civilization, known as the Old Kingdom, Thebes was little more than a small farming village on the banks of the Nile. It was only later that it developed into an important city. These Egyptian periods are known as the Middle Kingdom (2040 to 1730 B.C.E.) and the New Kingdom (1552 to 1069 B.C.E.).

The first rulers of the Middle Kingdom came from around Thebes and chose to make it the center of their new kingdom. The land around Thebes was plentiful and **fertile**. Thebe's location also allowed the new rulers to control both upper Egypt (upstream) and lower Egypt (downstream). The new rulers worshiped a local god called Amun-Re. Amun was the king of all Egyptian gods and was related to the Sun god, **Re.** The worship of Amun-Re soon spread across the state of Egypt, and Thebes became the spiritual center of Egypt.

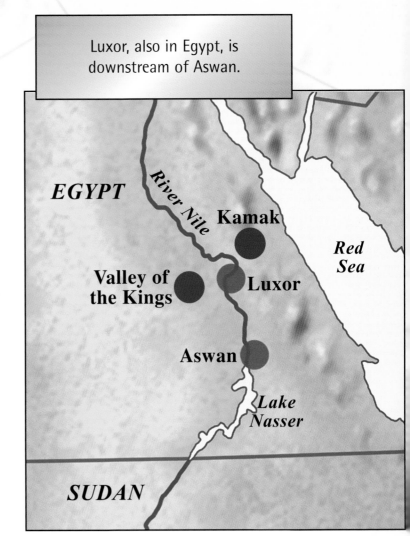

Luxor, also in Egypt, is downstream of Aswan.

The Nile runs through the middle of Luxor. The city is on one side with mountains behind it. The other side is mostly farm land.

The importance of religion

The Nile divided Thebes into two halves—eastern and western Thebes. Eastern Thebes was the city of the living. It was here that the Sun rose each morning, bringing new life to the river and its people. The **pharaohs** built great temples to honor Amun-Re and the life-giving Sun. On the opposite side of the Nile was western Thebes. Here the Sun would set each evening behind the cliffs that line the edge of the Nile valley. The Egyptians chose western Thebes to be the burial place for the dead. They believed that by burying their dead here, the Sun god would safely transport their dead into the underworld where they could have

eternal life. It is for this reason that western Thebes is often known as the city of the dead or the **necropolis** of Thebes. Western Thebes became the home of the priests and of the craftspeople who built the great **mortuary** temples of the pharaohs. The west bank was also an important farming area because it was in the flood plain of the Nile.

FACT

The temples of western Thebes were built over a mile (2 kilometers) inland from the banks of the Nile. This was to prevent flooding when the Nile overflowed each year.

17

Karnak Temple still has the remains of a canal at its entrance.

Temples of the Nile

In ancient times, the Nile connected both halves of Thebes. Boats carried people and goods between the two halves. Most boats would have been made of **papyrus,** because this was freely available along the banks of the Nile. The ancient Egyptians also built stronger barges for transporting heavy goods and for use in elaborate festivals. These barges were made of wood, much of which was imported from neighboring countries, such as Lebanon. These barges allowed the Egyptians to transport stone for building the temples of Thebes. Without the Nile, the temples may never have been built.

To move the stone as close to the temples as possible, the pharaohs ordered that canals be built. These artificial channels connected the temples to the Nile and had busy **wharves** on which building materials were unloaded from the river. The remains of some of the canals and wharves can still be clearly seen today.

In addition to being used to transport stone, the Nile itself provided an important building material—mud. Nile mud was made into bricks that were baked hard in the sun. These Nile bricks were used to build temples as well as houses. The main temple in Luxor is the temple of Amun-Re. This enormous temple is better known as the temple of Karnak. It is located alongs the Nile just north of the center of Luxor. As different pharaohs came and went over a period of 1,300 years, the temple itself underwent great changes. Some pharaohs tore down parts, while others rebuilt sections or added new ones. **Archaeologists** believe that most of the temple was built by the pharaohs of the New Kingdom, but parts of it date back almost 4,000 years.

This wall painting shows the Opet festival during the Nile floods.

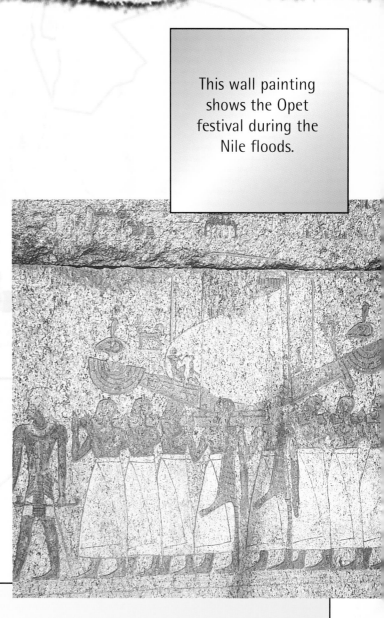

The Opet festival

The great city of Thebes owed its wealth to the Nile's life-bringing waters. Each year, the ancient Egyptians would celebrate this with the Opet festival at the peak of the Nile flood. The centerpiece of the festival was a showy sacred barge. The barge was used to carry a statue of the god Amun-Re from the main temple at Karnak to the Luxor Temple upstream. Here he was reunited with his wife, Mut (which means "mother"), and his son Khonsu, the god of the Moon and of healing. The festivities included dancing, acrobatics, flowers, and sacrifices to the gods. After a few days, the sacred barge sailed downstream again and Amun-Re was returned to his temple in Karnak. In another annual festival, Amun-Re was carried across the Nile to visit the temples of the dead pharaohs.

Tourist hotspot

The modern name for Thebes is Luxor. This name comes from the Arabic word *Al-Uqsur*, which means "the palaces" or "the castles." The name Luxor refers to the many fine temples and palaces that were built by the ancient Egyptians long ago. Today, these attract thousands of tourists to Luxor every year. Most visitors come to see the grand temple at Karnak and the famous Valley of the Kings. Here, the pharaohs of the New Kingdom were buried with great treasures for their eternal life in the underworld. Unfortunately, thieves robbed most of the tombs, and all that is left today are their beautifully painted walls.

> The Valley of the Kings has two parts, the East Valley and the West Valley. The East Valley has most of the tombs of the New Kingdom pharaohs and attracts more tourists.

2040–1069 B.C.E.	2000 B.C.E.	c.1550 B.C.E.
Era of the Middle Kingdom and New Kingdom. Thebes becomes an increasingly important city.	Earlier parts of the temple of Karnak are built.	The first Opet festival takes place.

One tomb did survive the thieves, and that was the tomb of Tutankhamun. This tomb was discovered in 1922 by British archaeologist Howard Carter. Inside the tomb, Carter found great treasures. Many were made of solid gold. The treasures made the Valley of the Kings famous and turned them into a major tourist attraction. The treasures are now on display in the Egyptian Museum in Cairo.

Today, tourism is the most important activity in Luxor. The River Nile is at the center of this activity. Nile cruise boats are among the most popular ways to see the Nile and the attractions along its banks. Luxor is a favorite destination for the cruise boats. Each cruise boat brings hundreds of new tourists into Luxor. During the busy season, the boats may line up several deep along the busy waterfront. Feluccas (see page 13) offer a more traditional way to cruise along the Nile. However, today few tourists travel in this way.

Whether the tourists arrive by train or by airplane, they bring welcome jobs to the people of Luxor. Many people who live in Luxor depend on tourism for their incomes. So, in many ways, they still depend on the River Nile, much as their ancestors did. Without the gift of the Nile, the pharaohs may never have built the great temples of Luxor, and there would be little for the tourists to see in this royal city.

c.1325 B.C.E.	c.747 to 645 B.C.E.	1922 C.E.
Tutankhamun dies in his late teens.	Thebes is capital of Egypt.	Howard Carter discovers the tomb of Tutankhamun.

Alexandria: Learning and Farming

Gateway to the Nile

Alexandria is located at the western end of the giant Nile **delta.** At one time, the Nile delta was part of the Mediterranean Sea. Over millions of years, the **sediment** carried downstream by the Nile filled in the delta region and pushed back the sea. Across the delta region today, this sediment is between 50 and 75 feet (15 and 23 meters) thick and is rich in **nutrients** brought down from the Ethiopian highlands. This makes the soils of the Nile delta the most fertile in Africa and some of the best farmland in the world. Since ancient times, **settlements** were established here to take advantage of its rich soils. The Nile delta remains the most important farming area in Egypt today, and is where most of the country's population live.

Alexandria, in Egypt, is at the mouth of the Nile.

FACT

Delta is the name for the Greek letter D. The Greeks gave this name to the end of the River Nile because it was triangular shaped, like a capital letter delta (Δ). The word is now used for all river deltas.

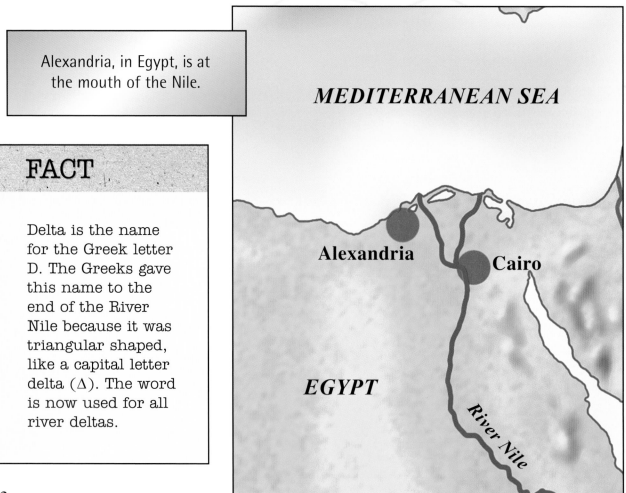

MEDITERRANEAN SEA

Alexandria

Cairo

EGYPT

River Nile

The Nile delta reaches inland for about 100 miles (160 kilometers) to a point just north of Cairo. Along the coast, it stretches a distance of about 155 miles (250 kilometers) between Port Said in the east and Alexandria in the west. Alexandria serves as a gateway between the crops of the delta region and the River Nile in general. The city is named after the Macedonian Greek conqueror Alexander the Great, who founded it in in 332 B.C.E. He conquered Egypt and chose the location of Alexandria for his new capital city. It was connected to the Nile by a canal and had a large natural harbor on the Mediterranean coast. This location made it an ideal place for trade between the people of the Nile valley and delta and the lands of southern Europe.

Alexander never actually lived in his city and died just nine years after founding it. He was returned to Alexandria, where his body was preserved in a glass coffin encased in gold. His tomb has never been found. After Alexander's death, the city was governed by another Greek ruler, Ptolemy I. Ptolemy was the first of many rulers to control Egypt and the River Nile during what is called the Ptolemaic era (323 to 30 B.C.E.). During this period, Alexandria grew into a large and wealthy city. The key to its success was its position as the gateway to the Nile. Within just one hundred years of its foundation, it was the greatest city of the ancient world.

The lands of the Nile delta are a fertile farming area that supply much of Egypt's food and many crops for export.

Paper, grain, and cotton

Alexandria is famous as an ancient center of learning. Much of this fame came about because Alexandria could obtain a form of early paper, called **papyrus.** Papyrus was made from a reed of the same name that grew alongside the Nile in the delta region. The stem of the reed was split into thin strips that were then pressed together and dried to form a single sheet of papyrus. Many of the ancient world's greatest scholars studied in Alexandria. These scholars included the mathematician Archimedes, who invented a device for drawing water from the Nile to water farmers' fields, and the geographer Ptolemy, who produced one of the earliest maps of the Nile.

The many documents created in Alexandria were stored in a great library. At its busiest, the library held some 700,000 papyrus scrolls. Unfortunately, most of this was lost in 48 B.C.E. when a fire destroyed the library.

This seal shows the grand buildings of Alexandria as they would have been at the height of its power.

332 B.C.E.	323–330 B.C.E.	48 B.C.E.
Alexandria is founded by Alexander the Great.	Alexandria grows into a large and wealthy city.	Fire destroys Alexandria's library.

The modern port of Alexandria is the most important in Egypt, handling 75 percent of all Egypt's foreign trade.

When the last of the Ptolemaic rulers, Cleopatra, died in 30 B.C.E., Egypt became part of the Roman Empire. Alexandria continued to be the capital of Egypt and to grow under the Romans. It became a center for transporting grain between Egypt and Rome. The Romans needed vast quantities of grain to keep their troops well fed. They came to depend heavily on the **granaries** of Alexandria and the Nile. This meant that Alexandria continued to be an important city until near the end of the Roman Empire.

In around 640 C.E., the Romans lost control of Egypt to Islamic forces from Syria. Al-Fustat, which was close to modern-day Cairo, became the new capital, and Rosetta became the main port. As a result,

Alexandria fell into a decline that lasted until the rule of Muhammad Ali (1805 to 1848). Muhammad Ali wanted to make Egypt into a great **maritime** power. He chose Alexandria as the country's main port. Most importantly, however, he built the Muhammadiyah Canal, which connected the city to the Nile. This happened during the start of cotton **cultivation** in Egypt. Cotton came from Pakistan and India and was introduced into Egypt by the British. The Nile delta region was well suited to growing cotton. The crop was shipped to the cotton mills of England and helped the city become prosperous. Today, Alexandria is the second-largest city in Egypt, with a population of around 6.5 million. It is a modern city that still relies heavily on its connections to the River Nile.

30 B.C.E.	**c. 640 C.E.**	**1805–1848**
Egypt becomes part of the Roman Empire.	Islamic forces from Syria take control of Egypt and Alexandria falls into decline.	The reign of Muhammad Ali, during which time the Muhammadiyah Canal is built.

Cairo: A Mega-city

City of the Nile

Cairo is a city built around the Nile rather than along it. Some parts of the city are even built on islands in the middle of the river. The earliest **settlements** in the area were small farming villages. Settlements similar to these still exist on the far outskirts of the city. The key to Cairo's growth was its special location on the river. Cairo is located at the meeting point of two **fertile** farming areas—the Nile valley upstream and the Nile **delta** downstream. Because the rest of Egypt is mainly desert, most people have always been crowded into the land surrounding the Nile. Cairo's position between these two areas made it a good location for controlling both the people and the trade of the River Nile.

Cairo, in Egypt, is the biggest city on the Nile.

The first major settlement in the Cairo region was at Memphis, which was located around 14 miles (22 kilometers) south of the present city center. Memphis was founded as the Egyptian capital around 3100 B.C.E. and stayed the capital city for about 1,000 years. It was from Memphis that early **pharaohs** built the pyramids at nearby Giza. Today, both Giza and Memphis are part of the Cairo urban area. During the later periods of ancient Egypt, Memphis lost much of its power to new capitals in Thebes (Luxor) and Alexandria. However, because of its position on the Nile, it always remained an important **administrative** and military center.

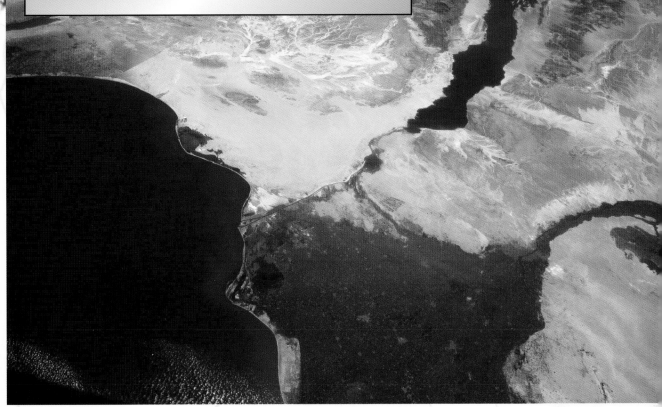

This satellite image shows the Nile delta in the bottom center and the Nile valley on the right. Cairo rests where these two areas join.

An Islamic city

The city of Cairo was founded in 969 C.E. by Islamic rulers known as the Fatamids. Muslims first controlled Egypt in 639 C.E., when Arabic conquerors defeated the Romans. The Muslims built a new settlement in order to control the Nile region. They called it Al-Fustat, which means "the **entrenched** camp." Under Muslim control, Al-Fustat quickly grew into a thriving commercial city. Within a few generations, Cairo had a population of several hundred thousand people. In 969 C.E., the Fatamids took control of Egypt. They built a new city outside of Al-Fustat and named it Al-Qahirah, which means "the victorious." Al-Qahirah is considered to be the start of the city of Cairo. Parts of this original city still exist today.

FACT

The name Cairo originates from Al-Qahirah. European traders mispronounced Al-Qahirah, and it gradually became known as Cairo.

The largest settlement

Cairo is by far the largest settlement on the River Nile. It stretches along the Nile for 20 miles (35 kilometers) and extends to the east and west of the river for several miles. In total, Greater Cairo, which includes the city center and its suburbs, covers an area of around 136 square miles (353 square kilometers). In 2003, the population of Greater Cairo was said to be at least 10 million people. This makes it one of the world's few mega-cities, or cities with more than 10 million people. Cairo is still a rapidly growing city. Because of this, some experts suggest that the true population of Greater Cairo may be closer to 16 million or even higher. Between 2000 and 2015, the city's population is expected to grow by at least 2 million people.

Cairo depends on the River Nile in many ways. Around two-thirds of its people rely on water supplies from the Nile for their drinking water. The water is taken to special treatment facilities to be cleaned and made safe for drinking. It is then piped into people's homes, and to shared public faucets in office buildings or on the streets. Water from the Nile is also used by Cairo's many industries,

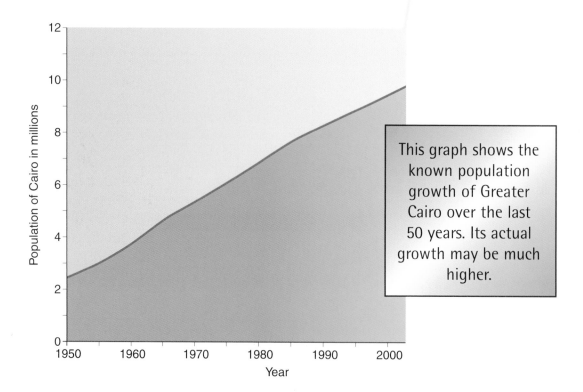

This graph shows the known population growth of Greater Cairo over the last 50 years. Its actual growth may be much higher.

This is an industrial district near Cairo. The Nile provides water, electricity, and transportation for industry.

such as textiles and the processing of food from the surrounding rural areas. In addition, heavy industries, such as engineering, steel, and chemical production are found in Cairo. Many of these industries have chosen to take advantage of the Nile water in their manufacturing processes by locating their factories on the riverside north and south of the city center. The river also provides them with a transportation route for raw materials and finished goods.

Not only does Cairo take water from the Nile, but it also also returns large quantities of used water back into the river. The water is often polluted with waste from homes, factories, and industries. This damages the river

FACT

The urban area of Cairo is the most populated settlement in Africa.

environment, killing fish and other river wildlife. This waste can also pollute the water supplies for people living further downstream. Since 1980, the Egyptian government has been working to reduce pollution of the Nile. They have passed laws that ban dumping industrial wastes in the river. Although this has improved the situation, much waste still ends up in the Nile. In the future, as Cairo's population continues to grow, this problem is set to get even worse.

Bridging the Nile

Before 1964, the annual rise of the Nile's waters often flooded the western bank of the Nile. Because of this, most of Cairo was built on the eastern side of the river, where the land was a little higher. After 1964, the problem of flooding was controlled by the construction of the Aswan High Dam (see pages 14 to 15). This opened up the western bank for development. A building boom soon followed. As the city expanded, thousands of new homes were built and small farming villages were quickly swallowed up. Today, the western side of Cairo is still growing. It stretches almost 12 miles (20 kilometers) inland from the Nile to the ancient pyramids of Giza.

A crowded river taxi crosses the Nile in Cairo. Cairo struggles to keep pace with its fast-growing population.

c.3100 B.C.E.	639 C.E.	969
Memphis is founded as the Egyptian capital.	Egypt comes under Muslim control.	Cairo is founded by the Fatamids.

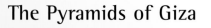

The Pyramids of Giza

Although the pyramids at Giza are surrounded by desert, they exist because of the annual flooding of the Nile. The floods covered much of modern-day Giza and brought the Nile almost to the foot of the pyramids. This allowed workers to carry enormous blocks of stone to the pyramids by boat. These stones included limestone from across the Nile at Tura and stone from quarries at Aswan more than 500 miles (800 kilometers) away. Scientists believe that it took at least 20 years and more than 20,000 workers to build each pyramid.

As the population of western Cairo increased, people needed a better connection across the Nile between east and west Cairo. This led to the construction of several new bridges. The most important of these bridges is the "October 6 Bridge," which was started in 1969. The bridge is unusual because after it has crossed the Nile, it continues into the heart of eastern Cairo as an elevated highway. The bridge handles about half of Cairo's traffic every day, or about 40,000 cars per hour. Also on the Nile, many ferries carry passengers across, up, and down the river. Because Cairo is so divided by its river, these forms of transportation make sure the Nile's greatest city will to continue to grow.

1964	1969	1980
Construction of the Aswan High Dam is started.	"October 6 Bridge" started.	Egyptian government begins to reduce the pollution of the Nile.

Khartoum: The Meeting of Rivers

The elephant's trunk

Today, Khartoum is the capital city of Sudan. However, it was once part of an area that was first controlled by Egyptions and was later controlled by the British. Khartoum is located on the Nile near two other **settlements**, Omdurman and North Khartoum. Together, these cities make up Sudan's largest urban center, which has a population of about 3.5 million. Although the three settlements have their own characteristics, they are often simply referred to as Khartoum. Khartoum is located where the White Nile and Blue Nile meet and flow as a single river for the first time. Khartoum takes its name from a piece of land shaped like an elephant's trunk that lies between the rivers where they join. The city's Arabic name, *Al-Khurt um* means "elephant's trunk." This name was later adapted to become Khartoum.

Khartoum's location at the meeting of the rivers makes it a key location for controlling movement up and down the rivers. Because of this, in 1821 the Egyptian army established a camp there. The camp quickly developed into a formal settlement. By the early 1860s, it had a population of about

Khartoum is located in central Sudan.

30,000. Khartoum also provided a good starting point for exploring the heart of Africa. Because of this, it became an important trading post where the trade in slaves and ivory became especially important. Khartoum was also the starting point for Samuel Baker's expedition to find the **source** of the White Nile in 1863.

Slaving on the Nile

During the mid-1800s, Khartoum was a major center for the African slave trade. Slave traders ("slavers") would leave Khartoum with up to 300 armed men and sail upstream along the White Nile. The slavers would raid nearby villages to capture people as slaves and then ship them back to Khartoum. The slavers would also steal or buy ivory from local chiefs. In a successful raid, a slaver might return to Khartoum with up to 500 slaves and up to 19,850 pounds (9,000 kilograms) of ivory. The ivory and slaves were sold to traders, who then journeyed across the desert to the Red Sea, or down the Nile to Cairo. Slavery on the Nile reached its peak in the 1860s. At this time, an estimated 15,000 Arab slavers were capturing 50,000 slaves a year from the lands of the upper Nile.

Battles on the Nile

During the last decades of the 1800s, Khartoum and Omdurman became the center of a power struggle between British authorities and an Islamic religious leader known as the Mahdi. The British had invaded Egypt and taken control of Khartoum. The Mahdi rose to power from a small island in the Nile about 150 miles (240 kilometers) south of Khartoum. He gathered support throughout Sudan and soon had a large army under his control. In March 1884, Mahdi's supporters approached Khartoum and attacked. Before the attack, British Governor-General Gordon evacuated about 2,000 people. However, Gordon refused to surrender to the Mahdi. The long siege began with Gordon trapped in his palace as he waited for support to reach him by the Nile.

In January 1885, after a 10-month siege, 50,000 Mahdi supporters launched a final attack on Khartoum. They killed Gordon along with most of the population of Khartoum. British reinforcements

The tomb of the Mahdi in Omdurman stands as a reminder of the power struggles that took place for the control of Khartoum.

This painting, of the battle of Omdurman, shows the Nile in the background.

arrived by steamer up the Nile three days too late. Khartoum had already fallen. The British came under fierce attack from the Mahdi's forces and retreated back down the Nile. The Mahdi built a new capital across the river from Khartoum in Omdurman. However, he died just a few months after this victory. Today, Omdurman's tomb is a site of pilgrimage for Muslims and a major attraction for visitors to the city.

The Mahdi was succeeded by one of his followers, Khalifa Abdullah. The Khalifa ruled from Omdurman for the next decade and continued to spread the beliefs of the Mahdi. In 1898, the Khalifa's rule ended when the British traveled up the Nile by steamboat. General Horatio Kitchener and his forces reached Omdurman on September 1, and quickly overpowered the Khalifa's forces.

As peace returned to the region, Khartoum was again declared the capital of the area. Soon, traders began to return and the city began to grow. Kitchener was given the job of rebuilding Khartoum. He laid out a city of wide tree-lined avenues that survive to this day. Many fine buildings were constructed during this period. In addition, a new industrial area began to develop in what became North Khartoum.

By 1902, Khartoum had also become a center of learning. It had its own college, which later became the University of Khartoum. Trade continued to be the main activity in Khartoum, and the Nile was used to transport goods. Textiles, leather-goods, and **gum Arabic** were among the region's most important wares.

35

The Gezira project

Today, the Nile is still an important part of Khartoum. This is because the city's economy still depends heavily on agriculture. The most important agricultural region in Khartoum is called Gezira. It is a large area of land south of Khartoum that is sandwiched between the White Nile and the Blue Nile. In 1911, the British began the Gezira project in order to grow cotton for England's textile mills. In 1925, workers built the Sennar Dam across the Blue Nile. The Sennar Dam redirected river water into a system of **irrigation** canals and to the fields of Gezira. The extra water led to a massive expansion of the project. When Sudan became independent in 1956, the Sudanese government continued the Gezira project.

By the 1970s, the Gezira project covered an area of 2.5 million acres. In addition, it provided water for more than 100,000 farmers who lived on the land. As the extent of the project increased, so too did the network of canals and ditches that carried water from the

This worker is letting Nile waters onto the irrigated fields of the Gezira project.

1821	1885	1898	1902
Egyptian army establishes a camp at Khartoum.	The Mahdi defeats the British at Khartoum. The capital is moved from Khartoum to Omdurman.	British forces overpower the Khalifa at Omdurman. Khartoum becomes the capital again.	Khartoum has its own college.

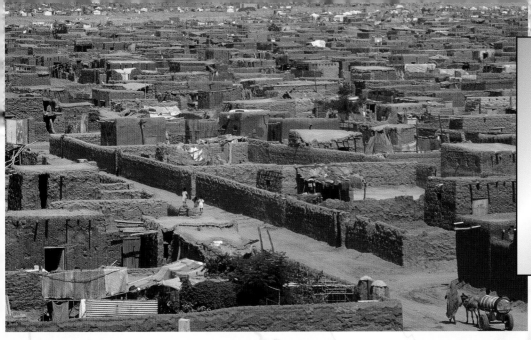

Refugees from countries suffering drought have fled to Khartoum, so the city continues to expand.

Blue Nile to the fields. Today, this network stretches for about 2,700 miles (4,350 kilometers). This makes it one of the biggest irrigation projects in the world. Cotton is still the most important crop grown on the Gezira project. The raw cotton is taken to Khartoum for processing and is then exported to markets around the world. Other crops grown at Gezira include peanuts, millet, sorghum, wheat, and different vegetables. Most of these are taken to markets in Khartoum to feed the growing local population. The Gezira project is one of the best examples of the Nile's great benefits. Without it, there would be less food available and the many industrial jobs that depend on Gezira would not exist.

City of refugees

During the 1970s and 1980s, Sudan and its neighboring countries suffered from many droughts and conflicts. These problems severely hurt food supplies in the region and led to terrible famines. Millions of people were forced from their homes to search for food and water, and hundreds of thousands died. Many refugees headed for Khartoum, and the city's population grew rapidly. At the start of the 1970s, Khartoum's population was 665,000. However, by the end of the 1980s it had increased to over 1.8 million. The Nile River was an important attraction for people, because even in the very worst of droughts the Nile continues to flow. Many of the refugees settled in Khartoum and have never returned to their homes.

1911	1925	1970-1980
Gezira project started by the British.	Sennar Dam built across the Blue Nile.	Refugees flood into Khartoum because of droughts in Sudan and neighboring countries.

Jinja: Source of the Nile

"A stone"

Jinja is located in Uganda at the point where the White Nile leaves Lake Victoria. The town depends heavily on the river and lake. They provide people with transportation, energy, food, and jobs. Even the name Jinja is related to the river. It come comes from the word *ejjinja*, which means "a stone" in the local Luganda language. The name is said to refer to a stone that stands close to Ripon Falls, which John Hanning Speke believed were the **source** of the Nile (see page 5). A plaque marks the spot where Speke is said to have made his discovery on July 28, 1862. Although later evidence showed that Ripon Falls are not the ultimate source of the White Nile, they are still important because this is where people can see where the White Nile begins its course.

Until the beginning of the 1900s, the area that is now Jinja was little more than a few fishing and farming **settlements**. At this time, the British controlled Uganda as part of their **colonial empire** in Africa. In 1901, they established Jinja as an **administration** and trading post.

Jinja is in Uganda on the edge of Lake Victoria.

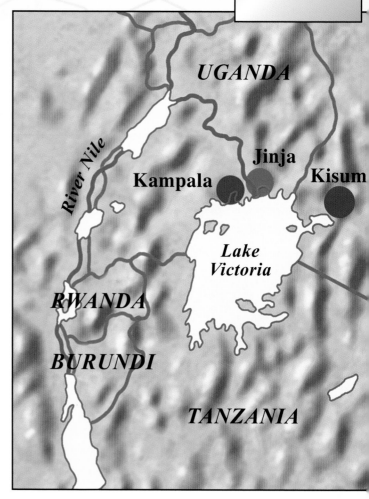

FACT

It takes about three months for the water entering the Nile at Jinja to reach the Mediterranean Sea.

38

Jinja soon became important to the British as a port for transporting Ugandan goods back to England. The goods were taken by steamboats from Jinja across Lake Victoria to Kisumu, in neighboring Kenya. In Kisumu, goods were moved by trains to the ocean port of Mombasa. Cotton and coffee were among the most important goods transported in this way.

THIS SPOT MARKS THE PLACE FROM WHERE THE NILE STARTS ITS LONG JOURNEY TO THE MEDITERRANEAN SEA THROUGH CENTRAL AND NORTHERN UGANDA SUDAN AND EGYPT

This plaque marks the spot where the source of the Nile was believed to be.

The East Africa Railway

*The East Africa Railway was started in 1896. It was part of an ambitious British plan to link Mombasa on the Kenyan coast to the **fertile** lands of Lake Victoria and the Nile. By 1901, the railroad reached Lake Victoria at Kisumu. In 1910, the British government extended the railroad from Jinja to Namisagali, a settlement located where the River Nile enters Lake Kyoga. This new railroad allowed workers to transport cotton grown along the Nile and around Lake Kyoga to the port in Jinja. Trade between the Nile region and Mombasa increased, and the government built a new section of railroad to connect Jinja directly to Mombasa in 1928. The East Africa Railway is still in use today. However, as road transportation became more popular, much of the railroad was abandoned and left to fall apart.*

The power of water

After the Owen Falls Dam was completed in 1954, Jinja grew rapidly. The dam was built a little more than a mile (about 2 kilometers) downstream of where the Nile leaves Lake Victoria. As the waters behind the dam rose, Ripon Falls were flooded. Today they are no longer visible. The main purpose of the Owen Falls Dam was to generate electricity for Uganda. As the water passes through the dam, it turns giant **turbines** that generate power. This is then transferred by power lines across the country.

Cheap electricity from the Owen Falls Dam as well as a plentiful water supply made Jinja a good place to set up factories. Jinja soon became the most important industrial town in Uganda. Since the building of the Owen Falls Dam, such industries as textile factories, iron **foundries, tanneries**, a sugar **refinery,** and a brewery have been set up in Jinja. These industries need large quantities of water and electricity as part of their production process. In addition, the dam itself is also an important industry. It provides electricity to Uganda and neighboring Kenya.

Water crashes through the Owen Falls Dam in Jinja.

1862	1896	1901
John Hanning Speke discovers the source of the Nile.	East Africa Railway started.	The British establish Jinja as an administration and trading post.

The Bujagali Falls in Jinja are sometimes used for white water rafting. They are threatened by plans for a reservoir.

The new industries provided jobs in Jinja, and this led to a growth in the town's population. By 2002, there were just over 100,000 people living in Jinja. Many thousands more live in the surrounding villages and travel into Jinja to work each day.

In 2001, a second dam was built along the original Owen Falls Dam. This helped to increase the amount of power produced. However, Uganda still suffers from a shortage of electricity. Because of this, there are now plans to build another dam across the Nile. The new dam will be located around 4 miles (7 kilometers) downstream of the Owen Falls Dam. The plans for the new dam are very unpopular with people living alongside the river. It is likely that their homes and land will disappear under the reservoir created by the new dam.

Jinja's location on the Nile attracts thousands of tourists each year. Most come to see the powerful force of the Nile as it cascades through a series of amazing rapids. Tourists can also challenge themselves by going white water rafting down the rapids. If the new dam is built, these rapids will be lost beneath the new reservoir. This could destroy the tourism industry in Jinja, which employs hundreds of people and is heavily focused on the Nile.

1928	1954	2001
New section of railroad links Jinja and Mombasa.	Completion of the Owen Falls Dam at Jinja.	Second dam built at Owen Falls.

The Nile of Tomorrow

The Nile is a truly remarkable river. Even though much of it flows through a land that is desert on either side, it supports millions of people. This is because some of the most **fertile** farmland in the world lies in Cairo, one of the Nile region's biggest cities. Nowhere is the dependence on the Nile more obvious than it is in Egypt. The ancient Egyptians connected their religion to the Nile, and thanked the river for their very existence. They based their entire lives around the Nile floods and the good fortune the river brought to their land. Though the force of the Nile is now controlled by the Aswan High Dam, the river still dominates Egyptian life. It provides Egyptians with water, power, and transportation. Without the River Nile, Egypt as we know it today would simply not exist. It is little wonder then that Egypt is often referred to as "the gift of the Nile."

People have been drawn to settle on the banks of the Nile since ancient times. Today, villages line its banks from **source** to **mouth,**

The Nile at Aswan still attracts people today as it has done for thousands of years.

but it is the big **settlements** that now dominate life on the Nile. The earliest of these settlements were built to control trade along the Nile. When these settlements were built, the Nile provided the only known route into the heart of Africa. The riches of gold, ivory, and spices that could be found there made control of the Nile one of the great prizes in the world. Civilizations and empires struggled for control of the Nile right up until the middle of the 1900s. The influences of the different empires and civilizations are obvious in the buildings and layouts of the Nile's settlements today.

But what does the future hold for the settlements of the Nile? As populations continue to grow, one of the main challenges will be to keep up with people's demands on the Nile's life-giving waters. People will need more water for their homes, for growing crops, for their industries, and for generating power. They will also produce more waste. And if this waste is not carefully handled, it could find its way back into the Nile and pollute its waters.

The countries of Uganda, Ethiopia, and Egypt all have plans for projects that use the waters of the Nile. These projects would reduce the amount of water that reaches settlements

Village life along the Nile continues in much the same way as it has for hundreds of years.

downstream. Some scientists have suggested that the Nile may soon dry up before it reaches the sea. Just as the Nile brought life to the people living alongside it, the river now depends on people to keep it healthy. The relationship may be changing, but the link between the Nile and its people is as strong as it has ever been.

43

Timeline

c.3100 B.C.E.	Memphis is founded as the Egyptian capital.
2613-2494	Pyramids at Giza are built.
2040-1069	Thebes (Luxor) becomes an increasingly important city.
2000	Earlier parts of the temple of Karnak are built.
1475	**Obelisks** transported to Luxor for the temple of Karnak.
332	Alexandria is founded by Alexander the Great.
323-330	Alexandria grows into a large and wealthy city.
30	Egypt becomes part of the Roman Empire.
c.639 C.E.	Egypt under Muslim control. Alexandria in decline.
969	Cairo is founded by the Fatamids.
1805-1848	The Muhammadiyah Canal is built at Alexandria.
1821	Egyptian army establishes a camp at Khartoum.
1860s	Slavery on the Nile reaches its peak.
1862	John Hanning Speke discovers the **source** of the Nile.
1863	Samuel Baker's expedition to find the source of the White Nile.
1885	Sudan's capital is moved from Khartoum to Omdurman.
1896	East Africa Railway started.
1898	British forces move Sudan's capital back to Khartoum.
1901	Jinja is established as an **administration** and trading post.
1902	First dam at Aswan completed by the British.
1911	Gezira project started by the British.
1922	Howard Carter discovers the tomb of Tutankhamun.
1925	Sennar Dam built across the Blue Nile.
1928	New section of railroad links Jinja and Mombasa.
1954	Construction of the Owen Falls Dam at Jinja.
1964	Construction of the Aswan High Dam is started.
1969	"6 October Bridge" started.
1970-1980s	Refugees from Sudan flood into Khartoum.
1971	Aswan High Dam completed.
1980	Egyptian government starts reducing Nile pollution.

Further Resources

Books

Banting, Erinn. *The Nile River Journey: The Nile*. New York Weigl Publishers, 2004.

Bowden, Rob and Maconachie, Roy. *Great Cities of the World: Cairo*. World Almanac Library, 2004.

Shuter, Jane. Life along the River Nile, Heinemann Library (Chicago), 2004

Park, Ted. *Take Your Camera to Egypt*. Raintree, 2003.

Using the Internet

Where to search
A search engine will look through the entire web and list all the sites that match the words in the search box. Try **www.google.com**. A search directory is a library of websites that have been sorted by a person instead of a computer. You can search by keyword or subject and browse through different related sites. A good example is **yahooligans.com**.

Search tips
There are billions of pages on the Internet, so it can be difficult to find exactly what you want. These search skills will help you find useful websites more quickly:
- Use two to six simple keywords, putting the most important words first.
- Be precise, only use names of people, places or things.
- If you want to find words that go together, put quotation marks around them, for example "St Anthony's falls" or "Gateway Arch".
- Going to the "cached" option of a result will highlight where the keywords you searched for appear on the website.

Glossary

administration/administrative
concerning management and control.
An administration center is a place
where decisions are made and records
are kept.

archaeologist scientist who finds and
examines evidence from the past that
is often buried in the ground

colonial empire group of nations,
areas, or peoples (the colonized)
ruled by one major power (the
colonizer). Britain had a colonial
empire until the early 1900s and
controlled large parts of the world
including Egypt, Uganda, and Sudan.

cultivation preparing and using the
soil for growing crops

delta area at the mouth of a river
formed by sand and soil being
deposited in a triangular shape

drought period in which rain falls
below what is normally expected. A
long period of drought can severely
affect farming and lead to food
shortages and famine.

entrenched establishing something
so firmly it is difficult for it to
be changed

erode the wearing away of rock and
soil by wind, water, ice, or chemicals

famine shortage of food that leads to
hunger and in severe cases may result
in death. Famine is often caused by
drought or by conflicts that disrupt
food supplies.

fertile rich soil in which crops can
grow easily

foundry building (factory) in which
metal is cast (made)

granary a storehouse for threshing
grain (separating off grain)

gum Arabic water-based gum from
acacia trees used as a glue and food
thickener

irrigation watering crops using
specially created systems, normally
used in areas of low rainfall

maritime having to do with the sea

mortuary building where dead
bodies are kept and prepared for
burial or cremation

mouth ending point of a river

necropolis ancient cemetery

nutrients substance that feeds
and provides the energy needed
for growth

obelisk square-sided pillar carved
into a pyramid shape at the top

papyrus a reed that grows in waterlogged land along the River Nile. Stems of the fully grown plants are used to make boats and the insides were used to make an early form of paper.

pharaoh king of ancient Egypt

Re Sun god and father of the gods. In ancient Egypt, Re was the creator of all life on earth and in heaven.

reaches sections of a river (upper, middle and lower reaches)

refinery a factory where a raw material, such as crude oil, is changed into other useful materials, such as gasoline

refugees people forced to flee their homes because war or natural threats such as drought, flooding, or earthquakes threaten their lives

sediment fine particles of soil and rock that are eroded (worn away) by the force of water and carried in a river or stream before being deposited farther downstream

Semitic family of languages from North Africa and southwestern Asia. They include the Hebrew, Arabic, Aramaic, and Maltese languages.

settlement place that has people living in it permanently. Settlements can vary in size from a small village to a large city.

source starting point of a river

tannery a place where animal skin is changed into leather

turbine a motor that is turned by steam or water

water table level in the ground. Below it the rocks and soil are filled with water.

wharf a level area along a river or sea to which a ship may moor to load and unload

Index